GW00382154

DESTINATION
ALGARVE

A classic rocky seascape in western Algarve: Ponta da Piedade near Lagos.

DESTINATION
ALGARVE

Photographs: Cornelius Weber
Ruth Engels · Jan Bode
Text: Ulrich Fleischmann

WINDSOR BOOKS
INTERNATIONAL

Praia da Vau. The rugged west coast is windswept and its seas rougher and cooler than the sandy beaches to the east.

CONTENTS

The city beach at Albufeira, its eastern section used as a night-time harbour by local fishing boats.

ON THE OUTSKIRTS OF A GLORIOUS PAST

Paths to the Sea

It is the last day of a package tour to Algarve. The return flight from Faro to London has been delayed by several hours. Having exhausted the meagre entertainment offerings at the airport, the English visitors, filled with anticipation of a British autumn, stand idly and confused in the doorway. All around are fields of stubble and thistles, small stands of pine and cart tracks. In the distance, a white building turns out to be a bar-restaurant, on the basis of a soft-drink billboard. Equipped with coats, umbrellas, handbags and urban footwear, the tourists, with their thoughts already set on home, step foot onto the country lane heading toward the inn and once again enter the hot world of southern Portugal, passing by farm labourers and a cart laden with corn.

One might think of this as a world of glaring contrasts, but that is not entirely an accurate appraisal. The peasants scarcely look up from their work as the tourists pass by. Nor do the local red wine tasters at the bar pay them any attention. The visitors' request to pay separately, a concept unheard of among the Portuguese, causes a bit of consternation, but the problem has been encountered before and is solved with a bit of time and paper. Faro International Airport, though set sheepishly off the main road, is not only accepted as an unavoidable aspect of modernity: it has turned Faro into a cosmopolitan capital and internationalized the surrounding area. It therefore seems to correspond with a tradition of Algarvean independence. For despite many efforts to push this nethermost corner of Europe into a picturesque marginality, Algarve has always been Portugal's birthright. Algarve is not simply Portuguese, much less only a Portuguese province, as the country's absolute monarchs and fascist dictators have tried to make it. The early kings of Portugal acknowledged the special status of the region which is isolated from the rest of the country by twin mountain ranges: they referred to themselves as "Kings of Portugal and Algarve". Perhaps the ancient quip that "Portugal stands with its back to Europe" applies doubly to Algarve, which stands with its back to Portugal! Separated from the populous centres of Lisbon and Porto by the sparsely populated Alentejo region and two impassable mountain ranges, Algarve is a one hundred mile/one hundred-sixty kilometre stretch of seacoast with a life and destiny of its own. The sea, of course, is paramount: it signifies endless expanses, openness, and paths to worlds beyond the watery frontier. The old 1,000 escudo banknotes still mention the "dois Algarves", the two Algarves, hinting that there are other areas waiting to be discovered hidden behind the coast. Algarve's marginality and isolation also emphasises its role as a bridgehead to new worlds when the frontiers are crossed. Hence, at many times during its past, this seacoast was a veritable melting pot, inviting and cosmopolitan. International airports and the appearance of strangely clad foreigners merely carry on a saga which began centuries ago.

Algarve's ocean is the Atlantic, in medieval times the end of the known world. This border is marked by a dynamic seacoast: the treacherous sandbanks of the beaches near Spain give way increasingly to steep and inaccessible cliffs, ending in the far west in a windswept cape of majestic inhospitality. The distinctive "sandy Algarve", extending from Albufeira to the east, and a "rocky Algarve" to the west, is more than the result of geological conditions. The zone of sandy beaches is a transitional region recalling, in many ways, a Mediterranean climate: warm nights, an enchanting natural environment, a communion of land and sea. To the Romans, Visigoths and Arabs, the area marked the extent of their continuing conquest and subjugation of the southern coastlands. The eastern Algarve especially retained close political and cultural ties to Seville; signs of this still can be seen in Silves, once a bastion of Algarve's Arab civilization. Even today, the modern border with Spain, extending along the Guadiana River and Estuary, is an uneasily defended frontier. True, there are no bridges, but during the tourist season, ferries allow for the invasion of thousands of cars in rapid

The thirteenth century chapel of Nossa Senhora da Rocha, west of Armação de Pêra. Inside are model ships made of wood as well as votive offerings from fishermen rescued at sea. The beaches on either side of the one hundred foot/ thirty-five metre cliffs are linked by a tunnel.

9

Left: Algarve's mild climate and plentiful water permit three or four harvests each year. The produce is sold at local markets, like this one in Loulé.

Right: The largest fishing seaport on the south coast of Europe is Portimão.

succession from the Spanish town of Ayamonte into Portugal's Vila Real de Santo António. Here the countryside is flat, hot and physically exhausting. Many people tarry among the gigantic holiday high-rises of nearby Monte Gordo and Praia Verde before continuing on into the more animated landscapes of western Algarve.

Silves: Dream City of the Moors

"Even as she did conceal the sun from my sight,
So may she remain concealed from the eyes of fickle
    fortune!
She knows full well she is a moon, I swear,
For who else but she could obscure the sun?"

The town of "Silb" or "Xelb" (pronounced "Shilb") was celebrated thusly, in the metaphor of a woman, by its eleventh century ruler and most renowned poet, Almotamid. Today's Silves was the capital of the Muslim region of "Al Gharb", meaning the west. There were many who praised this town, in poetry of the most delicate hues, as one of the most magnificent in the Arabian world. Literature belonged to the cult of educated refinement, a refuge from a fate that had

begun to befall the region in its struggles against the Christian tribes from the north. In 1095 the area around Porto and Cale (Gaïa) was bestowed upon Henry of Burgundy, a landless prince and crusader, in gratitude for his military victories. With the help of other crusaders who were constantly passing through his coastlands in search of skirmishes with the infidels, Henry set about extending his domain to the south: Lisbon fell in 1147, as did Faro, then known as Santa Mariya al-Harun, in 1249, the last Moorish bastion in Algarve.

By this time, Silb had been abandoned. This "city of enchantments", as it was lauded in the Arab world, possessed mighty walls that we still can walk along today, and it had cisterns over sixty feet/eighteen metres deep to collect water in case of siege. But its fame was not due entirely to its defenses: in the broad valley which can be surveyed from the town walls, the Moors brought agriculture to its zenith. Gigantic water-wheels known as "noras", some of them still in operation today, carried the precious water, distributing it in the rice paddies. The Moors introduced almond and orange groves, the processing of sugar cane and olives as well as lettuce and the carrot. Wealthy from agriculture and trade, the Moors attained a level of affluence that allowed them

May Day festivities in the mountain village of Alte, northeast of Albufeira. Folk festivals, often a mixture of pagan and sacred rituals, are the culmination of a strenuous daily life-style in rural Portugal and offer folk dancing and traditional music as well as food and drink.

to pursue science and the arts, not only poetry but also philosophy, mathematics, grammar and jurisprudence. The magnificent buildings that adorned Silb brooked comparison with the Alhambra in Granada. But all fell prey to the evangelical zeal of the conquerors.

Silb's enchantment was its culture, luxury and easy life-style, a secular splendour that already alarmed the fundamentalist Almoravid sect in the eleventh century. In their quest for a revitalization of Islam, a holy war was waged against the caliphs then reigning in Andalusia. The resulting civil war came at exactly the wrong moment, for it allowed the advancing Christians to play one side against the other. And added to these forces were the ships filled with crusaders from Denmark and Friesland, men who gladly came to the aid of the King of Portugal in return for the right to plunder the conquered city. Silb defended itself for forty-nine days before initially capitulating in 1189. Reconquered by the Moors, it ultimately fell to the Portuguese in 1242.

"Silb, my Silb, once thou wast a paradise". Poets bewailed the twice-ravished city. But why did the new Silves remain such a humble country town rather than becoming, as in Andalusia, a Christian centre erected on the glories of a Muslim past? The answer is found among the circumstances surrounding the

foundation of the state of Portugal. As long as the crusaders and Christian forces were advancing to the south, the king bestowed the newly conquered territory on knightly orders with the intention of rebuilding and settling the area and thus setting up a buffer zone against the hostile caliphates. In Algarve, however, the Portuguese had reached the sea: the reconquest of the west was completed and even mighty Seville was in Christian hands by 1248. In 1297, the boundary was drawn between Portugal and Spain; this border has remained intact to the present day, a unique phenomenon in the history of Europe. Portugal became the first European nation to have a permanently defined territory. The country then directed its attention to its heartland, to the cities of Lisbon and Oporto. The spoils of war to the south, which were distant and hard to reach, were largely ignored. It was enough to have triumphed over Algarve's suspiciously pluralist culture of Arabs, Christians and Jews. The Muslim south had been decapitated.

No members of the new feudal nobility settled in Algarve. The local Arab and Christian peasantry could, therefore, carry on their lives largely undisturbed. After the first great wave of missionary work had passed, even the process of Christianization in Algarve became

Continued on page 16

"In my mind, as in a sea devoid of time and space,
I see in darkness thy pallid features Returning.
The hour I know not, only that it shall come."

In *"Mensagem"* ("The Message", 1934), the only volume of poetry published during his lifetime, the greatest poet of modern Portugal, Fernando Pessoa (1888-1935), invokes a centuries-old Portuguese world-view centring on the figure of the "Rei Encoberto", the vanished but ever-present last heir of Portugal's Aviz dynasty, King Sebastian I (see page 28). According to belief, ever since that fateful day when his "Last Ship" (to quote the title of another poem) disappeared over

One of Portugal's most well-known modern poets, Fernando Pessoa, photo taken in 1914. Pessoa at age six. Pessoa's identity card.

the horizon of Lagos, the king has been waiting in an unreal time between history and eternity to return to Portugal; according to Portuguese beliefs, when Sebastian does return, he will fulfill the vision of the Old Testament prophet, Daniel, by ushering in the "Quinto Império", the fifth kingdom of God on earth.

In the ancient mixture of Portugal's Christian and Jewish mythologies, this expectation of the coming Messiah has taken on a strangely lifelike dimension by blending with actual history. Thousands of men have died in crusades to purify the world, especially in the northeast regions of Brazil where the myth for the coming of Sebastian was carried by Portuguese immigrants. But the myth also found an "intellectual" champion in the famous seventeenth century priest, António Vieira. As a missionary working in Brazil and elsewhere, Vieira promulgated the doctrine of "Sebastianism", a Portuguese

THE PROPHET OF THE VANISHED KING: FERNANDO PESSOA

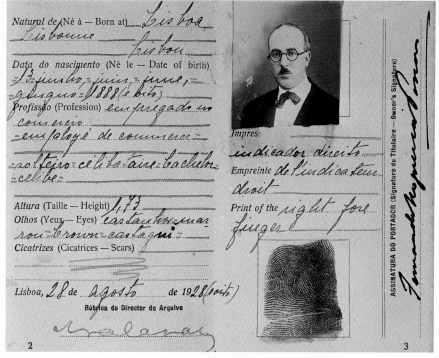

brand of messianism whose adherents wait passively, a trait characteristic of the entire Portuguese nation, for the coming of their saviour and redeemer.

Pessoa, then, was in good company with his cycles of poems on Sebastian and Henry the Navigator. But his images were carried further: their underlying ethos thrives on that Portuguese sense of "fado" which blends the fate of the nation with the private destiny of the individual. The "time and space" of the Sebastian myth, from the lines of verse above, lie within every Portuguese descendant.

"The sea had reached its destiny, the empire crumbled."

Deeds of history are but an episode in the infinity and eternity of nature. Those who perform and experience them partake of both: the finiteness of human action, and the infinity of longing.

These poems, which were translated into English and published by Penguin Books in 1974, should be read at Cabo São Vincente. Though Fernando Pessoa was not an Algarvian, there is perhaps no other poet who better captured the feelings of men caught between land and sea, between the known and the unknown.

Yet, in another volume in which he invented the poetic alter ego of Alvaro de Campos, a half-Jew from Algarve, he exposes these feelings as fractured and alien to our times.

The character of Pessoa-Campos bares his soul in an "Ode Marítima", depicting the symbiosis of man and sea in images bordering on hallucination. The hero is no longer the benevolent and redeeming Sebastian, but a cold-blooded pirate who flaunts every standard of morality. In the end, this vision of the omnipotent liberty of the sea vanishes, and Alvaro de Campos turns out ultimately to be a naval engineer intent on taming the oceans with modern technology, a reference to Portugal's Prince Henry the Navigator.

Returning from Cabo São Vincente to the modern Algarve of Albufeira and Faro, we can sense the truth behind this farewell to the heroic legends of the sea.

The fishing village of Ferragudo with its picturesque steps and alley-ways. Located at mouth of the Arade River, its sandy beach is ideal for children. The best view of the town and its fifteenth century castle is from the bridge linking Ferragudo with Portimão on the opposite bank.

A view from Alcoutim across the broad, gently flowing Guadiana River to the town's Andalusian neighbour, Sanlúcar de Guadiana.

lackadaisical and piecemeal. The resulting slightly mystical mixture of religion which came to characterise the region would later be attacked brutally but with limited success during the Inquisition. The local residents, notwithstanding some intermarriage with Flemish and Frisian crusaders, remained Muslim. Only gradually and sluggishly did they enter into Portuguese culture, instilling it in the process with Muslim traditions. Nowhere on the Iberian Peninsula are we as close to the Moors than in this southern part of Portugal, where the ancient water-wheels still turn, where the cubic white buildings recall northern Africa, where the flowering almond trees conjure up tales of Arabian princesses, and where the place names begin with the Arabic definite article "al". Isolated from trade routes and town markets, Muslim agriculture suffered but never entirely vanished.

Throughout its long history, Algarve has been the home of widely divergent cultures. This has left a mark in its people, language and architecture. Above: A shop in Vila do Bispo. Middle: Gypsies in Silves. Below: Over the centuries the North African style of architecture has been especially noticeable, as here in Fuseta.

Beyond the Edge of the World

To the Portuguese, "Sagres" first and foremost denotes a brand of beer, a brew so popular that in ordinary conversation the word is synonymous with beer itself. Sagres is also the name of the last tiny town in the west of Algarve. It is one of the few locations where the highlands do not end in steep sea cliffs, but leave room on the narrow coast for a few houses and access to a modest harbour that is crowned by an eighteenth century fortress. Surrounding this enclave is a countryside of utter desolation, a region separate from the beckoning green hillsides in the east. A cold wind continually blows over the plateau, stunting the sparse vegetation. This is a flat expanse of land carpeted by the agave plant which spreads its long, bare spikes toward the sky as it blooms. Again and again the red cliffs terminate in a mighty abyss tumbling down into a sea on which miniature ships can be seen wending their way. In the evening, accompanied by brilliant sunsets, an unexpected and almost unearthly cold begins to spread, causing unsuspecting tourists to clutch at their recently purchased wool pullovers. Until a few years ago there were almost no hotels here, and overnight visitors were wild looking creatures who slept in tents weighed down by rocks.

From Sagres there is a short path leading over the plateau to nearby Cabo São Vincente, the last outpost on the continent before the boundless expanse of the sea. This is the "end of the world". The uniqueness of this spot has impressed visitors for centuries. In ancient times, as the name Sagres implies, it was "promontorium sacrum", a promontory sacred in the ancient sense of being remote and isolated. Ordinary mortals were not meant to stay here, for this region, close

Special features of Algarvean architecture include square buildings, ornamental recesses known as platibandas and rooftop terraces. Especially on houses in Algarve towns, as here in Pêra, the patios are enclosed by balustrades and decorated with columns and figurines.

Cubic structures, often one storey high seem to echo Algarve's Muslim past. Yet most of these buildings are of recent construction. Fishermen and merchants imported this style of architecture, seen here in Estômbar, from North Africa during the late eighteenth century.

the setting sun, was the resting place of the gods. Supposedly at the edge of the world, presumed to be somewhere beyond the blue reaches of the sea, strange and dangerous beings cavorted, unchallenged by man. Similar to Cape Finisterre in Spain's Galicia, once Christianity was introduced, this became a site where the mortal remains of a long deceased martyr were miraculously washed ashore. In Algarve, it was Saint Vincent who gave his name to the cape; according to belief, Saint Vincent was brought to this lonely spot in the then Islamic Portugal by ravens. (Oddly enough, this myth is recounted by an Arabic chronicler!) The precious remains then awaited rediscovery in a tiny, inconspicuous chapel. Following the Reconquista, they were taken to Lisbon in the heart of Portugal, where they became nationally revered relics. Here, then, at Cabo São Vincente, the new Christian nation of Portugal came of age, at the same time, producing a patron saint capable of asserting the country's independence against the cult of Saint James in Spain.

It is thus only fitting that Cabo São Vincente should also have witnessed the beginning of Portugal's great age, the waning Middle Ages of the fifteenth century. The period centres around the curious figure of Prince Henry, known as "the Navigator", though in fact he never once went to sea. He earned his nickname for his familiarity with the techniques of seafaring which he transformed into a science. A romantic tradition maintains that Henry established a maritime "school" at Ponta de Sagres, a narrow strip of land situated between the town and a stormy cape. Here, in a much visited rectangular complex of ruins, he set up his desk at a window overlooking the sea, mingling the ocean view with visions of distant lands. The authenticity of the story is questionable, but history needs these firm locations lest it devolve into legend. The life and labours of Henry the Navigator left many traces on the coastline between Lagos and Cabo São Vincente. His school was most likely situated on the cape's plateau, on the spot occupied today by a giant lighthouse. What matters more importantly, however, are Henry's ideas which changed our world. Lacking reliable maps and implements, seafarers of the time sailed over established routes, the knowledge of which was the private property of the ships' pilots. Anything beyond these routes was considered unknown and perilous. True, fishermen sometimes ventured into officially uncharted regions in search of prey, and they were probably aware of foreign coastlands which they used as points of orientation for their journeys. But as

A street in Ferragudo. Recessed niches painted in blue, green, ochre and even black as well as sharply outlined windows and doorways are typical of Algarve, as is the coat of whitewash applied annually to ward off moisture and heat.

it served entirely different needs, this knowledge remained uncodified and inaccessible.

Prince Henry was well versed in the world of sailing. Having set himself up in Raposeira, a small country mansion between the cape and Lagos, Algarve's major seaport at the time, he proceeded to collect all available information. Knowledge long buried or difficult to access was studied, including ancient and contemporary writings by Arab travellers as well as the jealously guarded secrets of Italian and Catalan mariners. In any case, Portugal's salt-filled breezes were ripe for new routes of navigation. Unlike other dynasties, the ruling house of Aviz had consolidated its power and was not preoccupied in internal battles with the nobility. As early as 1415, a first foothold in Africa had been obtained with the conquest of Ceuta. But the Aviz dynasty was not intent on expanding its domain by conquering another Algarve. Its goal was to take part in the profitable spice trade, then dominated by the Arabs owing to their knowledge of travel.

Prince Henry was the product of several fortunate circumstances. No doubt he was an eccentric who preferred life in the most remote corner of Portugal to the goings-on at court. Yet he was also a descendant of the mighty ruling dynasty and a Grand Master in the powerful national order of the Knights of Christ. When he wanted to obtain information, be it officially or secretly, he had enough money and power to do so. He was able to retain experts to help in the sorting and compiling of centuries of seafaring lore in order to produce new nautical equipment and, above all, a new type of seaworthy vessel, the caravel. But more than anything, Henry could ensure that these new instruments and vessels were actually built, and that crews were found to embark on voyages along the unexplored west coast of Africa. His project was carried out in several small stages: the first expedition set out in 1441, while Portuguese ships finally reached the southern tip of Africa in 1488 from where they could then slip into the well-known Arabic seafaring routes. The path to India was now open. This was not all: the world had lost its borders and was now manageable and accessible. And the discovery of America was merely a matter of time.

Henry died in 1460, before he could witness the success of his enterprise. From our vantage point in history, his maritime expeditions seem clear and purposeful: he has been called a "visionary" and a "harbinger of the modern age". There are days, especially during the autumn storms, when the solitude

19

Continued on page 25

For the most part, Portugal fell in line with the dominant currents in European art. But there was one noteworthy exception, resulting from a unique interplay of historical forces. The age of major discoveries and easy money during the sixteenth century that gave the reigning king, Manuel, his nickname "the Fortunate" occurred during the waning Gothic period and overlapped with the Renaissance, a movement initially unwelcomed by the conservative Catholic countries of the Iberian Peninsula. During the void which followed the Gothic years, the

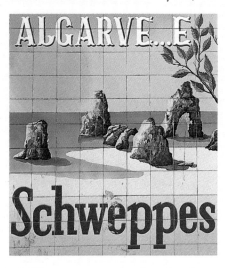

worldly Portuguese developed a desire for pomp and ostentation which would also be pleasing to God.

Traditional architecture in Algarve was also conditioned by two circumstances which complemented each other. Firstly, there was a lack of the natural stone that provided building materials in northern Portugal; and second, a skill was inherited from the Moors, the use of mud, lime, sand and water to make bricks or, after baking these elements with oxide dyes, water-resistant tiles. The tiles are frequently found around old springs and drawing wells, proving that the manufacture of glazed tiles survived the Reconquista by several centuries as a folk art.

Initially, the more affluent Portuguese purchased decorative tiles from the remaining Moorish principalities on the Iberian peninsula. In accordance with the Islamic faith, these *alicatados*, cut to size with special tongs, depicted no representational objects; at most, they presented ornamental figures in relief. This aspect changed with the expulsion of the Moors when the Portuguese themselves began to manufacture tiles. Two European traditions were also employed. The Italian majolica technique made it possible to paint freely on the tiles without

TILES AND CHIMNEYS

the risk of smearing the colours; large-scale murals were thu created. More importantly, however, was the spread of the Dutch tradition of Delft tiles during the seventeenth century. The familiar blue and white tints gave new character to the ancient Arabic "azulejos" (from *al-zulayi* meaning "little stone", combined with *azul*, the Portuguese word for blue). Originally the tiles were meant to protect the lower parts of walls from dirt. This function now gave way, especially during the Baroque, to an azulejo art in which entire walls of palaces and churches were covered with murals of tile. Algarve has an outstanding example of this type of art: the church of São Lourenço de Matos in the town of Almansil, situated on the road from Faro to Albufeira.

Another folk tradition, that of air-dried bricks, has remained more obscure, at least until recently. The artfully built chimneys (*chaminé*) in peasant kitchens not only provided a windproof channel for diverting smoke through openings

and gables, but also gave their owners a means of expressing their individuality. Bricklayers allowed the customer to describe his dream chimney, then asked for how many days of labour he was willing to pay. This determined the size and complexity of each individual creation.

One can still find many beautiful and striking chimneys built today as in days gone by hand. But the tradition has been largely undermined by the mass production of prefabricated chimneys which can now be bought at roadside stands or selected from a catalogue. Tourists in search of Portuguese fantasy have only to find a means of transporting these heavy and bulky items. Later, they can recall their adventures while seated at a log fire, in the warmth of an Algarve chimney.

The Church of São Lourenço de Matos in Almansil, with one of Portugal's most magnificent azulejo murals. The church survived the great earthquake of 1755 unscathed. The images in blue tile on the walls and ceilings, depicting the martyrdom of St Lawrence, were created by Polycarp de Oliveira Bernades in 1730.

Lagos, birthplace of the mariner Gil Eanes. From here, Portuguese ships embarked on their voyages of discovery and conquest.

Ponta da Piedade, an awe-inspiring natural wonder with a kaleidoscopic interplay of rocks and water. The grottos, caves, arches and tunnels of the coast are a paradise for diving, fishing and quiet contemplation.

Nestled between the Algarve's cliffs is a rich succession of small sandy inlets and beaches such as São Rafael, near Albufeira. The bizarre rock formations and grottos of Ponta da Piedade are best viewed from a boat; excursions depart daily from the Fort de Bandeira in Lagos.

and isolation of the cape plateau make it grand and awesome. The omnipresent swarms of tourists are gone, the kiosks with woolen pullovers and caps dismantled. All that remains are the wind, the cliffs alongside the surging sea, the rhythmic flashing of the lighthouse. The flux of history is transfigured in these moments and leads us to ask quite different questions. What did Prince Henry really know? Was he aware of the shape of the earth and the presence of continents beyond the seemingly infinite desolation of the seas? How did he overcome the medieval fears that beyond the visible horizon lurked regions where there was no wind, where the waters boiled, congealed or tumbled into an abyss? It had taken nearly fifty years to reach the southern tip of Africa, for no captain dared to venture more than a short distance beyond his predecessor. On the ship's return, the reports helped Henry's school add another page or two to its book of routes. In the end, it was discovered that the forces of nature are universal and that the laws governing navigation are the same everywhere.

From "Fatum" to Fado: the Portuguese Destiny

Rounding the Cape of Good Hope was only the first step in reaching the Far East. Portugal invested everything it had on this possibility: money, ships, men. Mercantile offices were set up in India and Malacca, Sumatra and Borneo, Timor and the Spice Islands. Once again Christian zealots were soon to follow, waging war with cities and sultanates that previously had only to deal with Arabs. Tiny Christian settlements were established that have survived to the present day as curiosities. In 1542, the "ships of Christ" reached Japan. The sailors brought back a strange item: paintings by Japanese artists depicted, in their own style and understanding, the arrival of outlandish bearded men with long noses. Everything the Japanese noticed about their foreign visitors was captured in caricature in these "namban" paintings, some of which are on display in Lisbon's Museum of Early Art. The details include the tall hats and parasols of the Portuguese; their manner of working the rigging of their ships is rendered as artistic but meaningless feats of acrobatics.

But also included in the images of the Portuguese retinue are men of definite African origin! How did Africans come to Japan? If at all, this almost forgotten story can be traced to Algarve. Portugal was a mercantile nation. Its expeditions were intended to bring back not only new knowledge but also a profit. This was especially true of the long era prior to the

Idyllic beaches removed from the flow of tourists, such as this one south of Lagos, have become a novelty.

development of the spice trade with India. The first ships to open the sea route around Africa were told to bring back whatever seemed useful and profitable. Their logs and chronicles unashamedly describe their tactics: wherever Africans were encountered on the lonely coastlands, they were overpowered and dragged onto the Portuguese ships. This opened a chapter in colonial history which lasted well into the nineteenth century, namely the trade of black slaves, who laboured on the Portuguese caravels and were transported to Europe by the tens of thousands, long before the discovery of America. Within a few decades, Lagos, the city of Prince Henry, grew from a tiny fishing village into one of the largest mercantile centres of the world, a warehouse and headquarters for the royal monopoly, the "Casa da Guiné". From 1441 it was also the major exchange for that most profitable of all commodities, human beings.

Even today, local residents claim the tiny harbour still groans during moonlit nights under the weight of the sufferings of those who passed through. The business transactions that ultimately sent these people to all parts of Europe took place in a squat building surrounded by columns and enclosing a courtyard. The statistics do not recount what then became of the Africans. Some escaped their dolorous station and entered European history and literature. The majority, however, vanished, leaving behind a few genetic traces that remain to be seen primarily in Portugal and Algarve where their numbers must have been great.

Later, as trade with India took on a greater significance and the Casa de Guiné was subordinated to Lisbon's "Casa da India", Algarve would be the last region in Portugal to benefit from the great riches brought in by the caravels bearing the red cross of the Knights of Christ. The mighty merchant fleets embarked and returned via the mouth of the Tejo River in Lisbon. It was in this city that King Manuel, who typified his age with the nickname "the Fortunate", erected those great churches and monasteries immortalizing his name. Manueline is the term given to the fusion of late Gothic styles and exotic elements brought to Lisbon by artists and sculptors from around the world. Manueline monuments in Algarve are rare and unspectacular. Still, Lagos remained an important outpost of the power centres in Lisbon. Together with Ceuta in northern Africa, and Arguim and Santiago on Cape Verde, it was a base in the network of African trade routes. Accordingly, Lagos has a few Manueline churches and monuments.

One of these, a window with Manueline decoration located diagonally opposite the slave market, became a symbol of Portugal's last major expedition, a voyage that climaxed in a military fiasco and ended the era of medieval Portugal as a sea power.

The date was 24 June 1578. Standing at the aforementioned window is a young man characterised by dream-like boyish looks, as captured in a portrait which how hangs in the Lisbon Museum of Early Art. He is Sebastian I, the last heir of the declining royal dynasty of Aviz and Portugal's final hope of retaining and expanding a global empire. With this thought in mind, Sebastian surveys an army of enormous size for its time: 15,000 infantry and 2,500 cavalry are preparing to embark on 800 sailboats with the aim of conquering a second Algarve in northern Africa.

The conclusion of the mission was decisive, spectacular, and remains shrouded in mystery. Fewer than seventy soldiers returned via indirect routes, crazed with thirst, hunger and fear. They told how Sebastian's army had been misled by false information and how it had lanched an attack into the searing badlands of Ksarel-Kebir. With their heavy metal armour and clumsy baggage train, the Portuguese troops fell to the mercy of the mobile Muslim cavalry. The army was dispersed and massacred in small units while its survivors were sold into slavery. None of the witnesses could provide a coherent picture of the battle, and most of all, none had seen Sebastian fall.

An entire nation waited for the return of its vanished king, the guarantor of Portugal's future existence. Unreliable and confused witnesses claimed to have met him as a slave, others had seen a lone wanderer on faraway coasts. Imposters and fanatics posed as emissaries of the king and even as Sebastian himself. But no one could advance a worthy claim to the throne. Eventually, as a result of complicated agreements and the bonds of kinship, the Portuguese throne passed to Spain. For sixty disastrous years, until the Wars of Restoration in 1640, Portugal disappeared from the stage of world events. Its network of trade relations and mercantile headquarters either withered away or was destroyed while the debts mounted by the king for his campaign left the country impoverished. Portugal became a neglected province of its former Spanish rival.

With this amalgamation, Algarve dropped from history for the second time. Lagos, once the mighty seaport of southern Portugal, had lost everything: its ocean-going vessels, its slaves, its king. Bereft of importance as a commercial seaport, its role as a remote fishing village was resumed.

And this is how we know it today, with a friendly, provincial manner which entices to its ancient city walls some of the tourists from the eastern seaside resorts. Next to the mighty sixteenth century fortress

Salema, a small fishing village near Sagres. Here, as everywhere on the Algarve coast, fishing is a year-round activity. The majority of fishermen continue to use traditional techniques while declining yields in the coastal waters have led some to the tourism industry.

Flowering almond trees in Silves, once the legendary cultural and spiritual capital of Moorish Al-Gharb. Today it is a quiet little town with few traces of its former wealth. Whatever remained following the plunder by crusaders during the siege of 1189 was destroyed in the 1755 earthquake.

and along the Avenida dos Descobrimentos, colourful fishing skiffs bob in the water with their nets flung out. On the grand central square, the Praça da República, near the statue of Henry the Navigator, peasants take a quiet break and lunch on coarse white bread, cheese and olives following their visit to town. Many of the men from the countryside have gone to sea or emigrated. Some have simply disappeared, others have become rich, a few return as strangers, remembered and yet forgotten. History has no forward impetus here, no urge to continue. There is something cyclical but yet self-defeating to the motion, like waves that swell and roll, only to collapse into nothingness. What largely remains for these people on the rim of the ocean is to muse and wait. They are left with their "fatum", from the Latin meaning blind fate, celebrated in the music of the "fado". Their sadness and yearning is manifest in that national cult of melancholy known as the "saudade". There is a quiet desperation that comes from knowing one's wishes are destined never to come true.

The Modern Age

Twice more in its history, the tiny nation of Portugal was swept upwards by the forces of progress and then allowed to collapse. The eighteenth century saw the long-awaited discovery of gold, silver and diamonds in Brazil. The "minas gerais", worked with slave labour, sent a surge of money back to the mother country. Portugal's churches, built at the time in the fashionable Baroque style, were extravagantly and sumptuously adorned with gold. The end of this era accompanied the arrival of Napoleon's troops, who plundered both the sacred and the secular. The royal family fled to Brazil, precipitating the loss of the colony.

A remnant of Portugal's colonial empire remained, allowing the country to play the role of world power in this century. These were the colonies of Guinea, Angola and Mozambique in Africa, and Goa, Timor and Macao in Asia. All were exploited and bitterly defended by the Fascist dictator Salazar. A few large companies and families profited from the colonies but certainly not Algarve, which again merely supplied the manpower: emigrants, seamen, and above all, soldiers.

Yet amid these changing fortunes, Algarve found a tiny niche in which it could set out on its own and develop into an outpost of enlightenment and modernity. This was the result of a single resource found here in great abundance, fish. The Carthaginians, and later the Arabs and Sicilians, valued the fishing

Silves later developed into a centre for the outlying agricultural region and for cork processing. A lively fair is held every year from the end of October to the beginning of November. The town is well worth a visit, especially as a starting point for excursions to the nearby Serra de Monchique Mountains.

grounds off the Algarve coast as they are ideally located on a route the shoals of fish travel during their annual migrations between the Atlantic and the Mediterranean. Catches were, therefore, not only large but predictable. They were also diverse, ranging from the tiny sardine – the staple of the Portuguese diet – to the species with the greatest commercial potential, tuna. Every year between April and June, the tuna, fat and heavy with spawn, migrate into the Mediterranean, only to return emaciated in July and August.

In early days, when trade routes over seas and mountains were difficult and time-consuming, the greatest problem was how to transport these perishable goods. Small species of fish could be smoked; others were spread on long wire frames to dry, a practice still used today. Once preserved, fish were a much-coveted commodity and hence an attractive source of income for the Portuguese crown. In 1773, a "Companhia Geral das Reais Pescarias do Reino do Algarve" – the royal fisheries of Algarve – took charge of the fishing industry. These were remarkable times. Lisbon had discovered the notion of an absolutist, enlightened and omnipotent state, a philosophy that led the Marquês de Pombal, Portugal's equivalent of France's Cardinal Richelieu, to become the great revitalizer of his nation.

Lisbon had been destroyed by the Great Earthquake of 1755. Pombal rebuilt it as a "rational" city; the lower town (Baixa), with its straight streets and rectangular intersections, reflects the practical ideas of the Enlightenment. But Algarve was also affected by the earthquake: its few towns along the Spanish border including Castro Marim and Cacela were devastated. Invoking the newly found authority of the state, Pombal used the disaster to open up the sparsely inhabited southernmost border region along the Guadiana River, till then a hotbed of smuggling, and place it under state control. The swamps in the Guadiana delta were drained in 1774, and within a mere five months there arose Vila Real de Santo António, a duplicate of Lisbon's Baixa. The town was meant to be the hub of activity in eastern Algarve, with a military base, customs office and the headquarters of the royal fisheries, complete with harbour and processing plants. Instead of the alleyways, courtyards and cul-de-sacs that make Portuguese towns so picturesque and confusing, Vila Real was given a large central plaza and streets running on parallel axes.

Vila Real became a monument to the Enlightenment but was somewhat less than successful. The fishermen living a few miles to the west, in Monte Gordo, had their own harbour and refused to move to this strange-looking town. There was also no desire to subordinate their livelihood to the royal monopoly. There was no market for Portugal's crafts and industry, and royal officials lived in a form of self-imposed exile. When Pombal fell from grace a few years later during the reign of Maria I, his experiment was forgotten. The ghost town was not rediscovered until 1879, when a fishing magnate from Genoa, using Italian machinery and expertise, set up shop in one of the empty buildings. Tinned tuna became a lucrative business, and a few local entrepreneurs followed suit and started tinning sardines as well. The area along the river front was filled with the din of equipment and the stench of fish; the harbour revived, and in 1906 the town obtained a rail link. A century behind schedule, Pombal's vision was coming true.

But as the Portuguese had learned from their history, the crest of every wave is followed by a trough. Today Vila Real is deserted save during a few months in summer when tourists cross the Guadiana between Spain and Portugal. The centre of town is no longer the plaza envisioned by Pombal but the Avenida along the river, where visitors can make their first and final purchases or pass the time drinking coffee with bagaço, the Portuguese grape liqueur. Occasionally some of the tourists venture into the interior of the town, which has scarcely grown beyond Pombal's original street plan. Here they are met by a museum-like atmosphere: buildings from the two boom periods are neatly laid out, with horse-drawn carriages and donkey carts rattling past. One can easily make out the buildings of abandoned canneries by their inscriptions and grand names that once were famous around the world: Angelo Parodi, Ramirez, Cappa. What has become of the tuna? Although fishing is strictly regulated and the migrating fish are now protected during the spawning period, their number has drastically declined. Many of the remaining shoals prefer to make detours around the hectic Algarve coastline.

Beyond History

Algarve means sunshine and beaches, dream holidays with a touch of folklore. It means architectural wonders situated between Vale do Lobo and Vilamoura, where the roads are dirt tracks dotted with concrete, a product of the avarice of international investors. It implies yacht harbours and golf courses, the resort of people who are often reminded which country they are in by looking at the name on the currency. And endless orange groves, the edges stacked with crates of fruit waiting to be picked up by twisting lines of tractors as well as summer

traffic jams between Faro and Albufeira. Algarve is a land on the periphery, a transit route, the domain of foreigners.

If the main coastal road is tied up with traffic, you might consider turning off to the north and seeing what the countryside behind the seacoast has to offer. First comes an area of densely populated and well-tended farmland, "o interior", as the locals call it. Silves is here, as are other towns and villages such as Loulé and São Bartolomeu with their Manueline churches. Time and luck permitting, you might discover a village festival in distant Querença, a very leisurely affair with a neighbourhood market and processions circling through the town plaza. Here there is always enough time, seated in front of a café and served with the local red wine, to watch the wooden stage being set up.

Then come narrow roads, rimmed with walls of white stone, almond trees and cypress, occasionally a farm or chapel, awkward and white, its doorways and cornerstones painted in an inimitable violet-blue. Nowhere does this colour have the same effect as in the hot air and blue skies of Algarve. In more arid landscapes such as the Serra de Espinhaço de Cão ("dog's spine") to the west, you can see entire fields of cactus with fruit ranging from green to dark red-orange; anyone who knows how to deal with the hair-thin prickles can pick them. You will be surprised how quickly the activity of the coast subsides into a venerable rural solitude, although some package tours, anticipating the frenzy of the coast, have begun offering "safaris" into the Portuguese "wilderness". In Milreu, with its Roman ruins, things are a bit more crowded. A few of the more curious may find their way to nearby Estói, to be surprised by a remote and miniature late eighteenth century palace. It was built by the Counts of Carvalho, who equipped it with gardens, fountains and Baroque statues. But you will usually find yourself alone in the enchanted gardens which are now falling into disrepair. A guard who has set up a cot in a tiny outbuilding soon appears and informs you, depending on his mood, that the interior which you are trying to look at through the shuttered windows is either completely empty or full to overflowing with choice works of art.

Those who prefer water landscapes will not leave Algarve unimpressed. Somewhat higher and more distant is an entire chain of impressive reservoirs, reachable via tracks with signs pointing to the "barragem" (dam). And after the swarms of bathers splashing on the coast, these reservoirs are a welcomed relief: pine woods extend to the shoreline, clear, dark green water, translucent all the way to the rocky bottom. Many of the dams have adjoining parking lots, remnants from

The enchanted but dilapidated gardens of the Counts of Estói, surrounding an eighteenth century palace. Roman mosaics created in nearby Milreu, benches of azulejo tiles, pavilions, Rococo fountains, Italian sculpture, busts and balustrades all combine in various stages of decay to convey a touch of transience and mortality.

The hub of Portugal's tuna industry is Tavira, a tranquil little town with a Moorish flavour situated at the mouth of the Gilão River.

Something is always in bloom in the Serra de Monchique, the garden of Algarve. Owing to generally clement weather and an abundance of water, the area is resplendent with middle European, Mediterranean, subtropical and even tropical vegetation, creating a paradise for beach-weary tourists.

the days of construction. With the proper equipment they often serve as campsites. Portuguese families, who traditionally spend the hot summer days near the water, tend to avoid the crowds of the Mediterranean beaches. But at the inland lakes, entire groups of friends and families can pitch their tents, occupying large areas with their temporary households. Even the valued hen sits nodding under the car, in the protection of the shade.

A little farther on the hills gain altitudes of 1,800 feet / 600 metres. Those who crave drama and adventure will find the isolated granite plateau of the Serra de Monchique, with its wild canyons and scenic lookouts, much to their taste. But you also may find yourself caught in a rainstorm from the clouds which cling to the high peaks. The cool temperatures, abundance of water and elevation have created a special kind of vegetation, flourishing in regions where the hand of man has not intervened. Dense undergrowth surrounds the evergreen oaks and chestnut trees. Now and again you can find the strange "medronheiro", whose fruit, the "medronho", is used to produce a popular, if acrid, liqueur. An enquiry into the dictionary will puzzle the botanically-minded, for "strawberry tree" is the English term for these woodland giants, no doubt because of the shape of their fruit.

A rich supply of water from clear streams and springs has given tiny Caldas de Monchique its reputation. The village is located on the "caldas", warm water springs known already in Roman times. It is actually not just a thin trickle of water but a gushing torrent from five different sources which promises relief from every imaginable discomfort. Still, the great age when upper-class tourists "took the waters" has gone, and all that remains are the grounds and casino. Those who stay here today must take pleasure in a nostalgia for past grandeur, or in walks through the woods along cart tracks and narrow footpaths. This is to experience Algarve from an entirely different angle.

A few miles up the road we reach Foia, the highest granite peak of Algarve with an altitude of some 1,900 feet / 902 metres. Frequently wanderers are accompanied by strips of clouds, obscuring the view in mists. But on clear, hot Algarvean days, the view is breathtaking. From one angle, you can see to the green desert of Alentejo, sometimes even as far as Arrábida, the peninsula adjacent to Lisbon. From the other side of the mount, you can look down on Portimão and Lagos and the pale blue shimmer of the sea, which for Algarvians, with their tortuous history, has been not so much a border but their ordained destiny – fatum.

In addition to fishing and tourism, agriculture is Algarve's major industry. Southern Algarve owes its fertility in part to an irrigation system set up by the Moors, with water-wheels called "noras" and narrow masonry channels on stilts. The vivid colours here are in the vicinity of Alcantarilha.

FIGS, FLOWERS AND ALMONDS
Accounts and Descriptions of Algarve

The texts included in the following anthology portray Algarve from a variety of angles. They provide insights into the daily life-style of the residents and recreate the experiences of travel during decades long past. Through the eyes of two Algarvean writers, the mysteries of fishing are explored. While the more well-known writers and travellers have tended to ignore Algarve and remain in Lisbon, we hope our selections demonstrate the pleasures awaiting us all in the humble and too often forgotten southern extent of Portugal, Algarve.

The Algarvian Personality

The image that is evoked by the word *Algarvian*, one of vitality and color, is based upon the quality of life that has developed in the lowland areas of the province. Seeing it for the first time, one is struck by the polychrome scene; on the roads are brightly painted carts drawn by sleek mules, their harnesses decorated with metal and colored designs. Even the rope which reaches under the mule's forequarters to hold down the shafts is of brightly dyed henequen fiber, and as if all this

were not quite enough color, long red and green tassels are hung on either side of the animal's head. Forming a backdrop for this traffic, white rock and plaster walls, carefully maintained and frequently calcimined, border the roads. Behind the walls, or facing directly upon the roads, are immaculately kept houses, painted in one or more of a great variety of colors, and topped by the pride of the Algarvians – fretted, lacelike chimneys.

First coming to it, one immediately realizes that he has entered a unique culture area; it has no duplicate.

The dispersal of houses throughout the countryside is in contrast to the urban concentration typical of its neighbors. In the clear air of the bright, dry climate, these scattered Algarvian homes glisten in white or colors. Their owners, who for the most part live in them and work the land around them, are proud of appearances and are frequent painters; calcimining is usually done by the woman of the house, who uses a palmleaf brush on the end of a long chestnut pole. They favor a bright color, either for the body of the house or at least for a trim; the solidly white house of Spain is not the rule here. Pride in appearance is reflected also in the care given to the walls and the garden. However, it should not be assumed that the women of the Lower Algarve are overburdened. The time that they spend on their houses and gardens is available because of a prosperity lacking in most parts of Portugal and Spain. Their position is in sharp contrast with that of the women in adjacent areas.

There is no shoelessness. Most women seen on the country roads are not walking, but are riding donkeys; most men are driving mule-drawn, two-wheeled carts. Women are ordinarily not burden carriers. Burdens are carried either by the numerous donkeys or by the mule-drawn carts.

As part of a university research project, DAN STANISLAWSKI, visited Algarve in the process of discovering the personality of the country.

Afoot in Silves

It's perhaps a mile from the little branch station, and you drive to the town in a curious kind of two-wheeled cart with a tilt. I hadn't a notion where my cart was going, and in fact didn't know whose cart it was. But when I got in on general principles, the man seemed to understand and whipped up his mule. You go through groves of what I think from their blossoms may be orange trees, and then up one hill and down another, and over a queer old bridge and there you are. And the driver was pointing at some steps that led apparently up into a barn. But it turned out to be the hotel, and though the women couldn't understand a word of either my French or my two-days-old Spanish, she did understand when I pointed to my mouth for food and put my head on my arm for a bed. And, laughing quite heartily, nodded assent. The Portuguese, by the way, were always laughing at me. They weren't a bit like the Spanish, who were a much graver people, I thought. Or perhaps it was my Spanish that made them grave. …

Who the people may have been who welcomed me at Silves I do not know. But there was a welcome. For the news of the Englishman's arrival seemed to spread like wildfire, and in a very few minutes two gentlemen were waiting at the little inn for the honour of my company when I had finished eating. They had a little French, and even a scrap of English. Then they introduced me to other gentlemen with no linguistic advantages at all, and, before I quite knew where I was, I had been made a sort of honorary member of the little club, and had been presented with everybody's visiting card. Everyone in Portugal seemed to carry a card, and I must have collected almost hundreds of them. It reminded me that for thirty-five years or so I've been meaning to buy some myself. I was even presented to a gentleman who seemed to be the Mayor, and he took me round the town's little electricity works, and turned on some extra wheels for my special benefit. Now that's a pretty compliment that the Mayor of Hornsey has never paid me.

From that Square of theirs where the Mosque-Cathedral stands you get rather a wonderful view. The little town lies flat-roofed below you in regular steps, and the girls with their water-pitchers crooked into their brown arms are gossiping in the cool of the evening exactly as the Silves girls must have gossiped back in the fourteen hundreds or whenever it was that they put up that *Cruzeiro*. There was a one-legged crippled boy playing on the stones just in front of the Cathedral Door. Then down at the very bottom of the valley runs the Arade River, and in the crystal-clear light of the Southern dusk it gleams exactly like silver. And with the heat of the sun abated at last, the people have lit their fires and there is cooking smoke from every chimney in the valley. Then when even the dusk had gone and it was quite dark, we were all walking in a sort of garden that they took me to. About a dozen of us in a double line, with the two who could understand a bit of French on either side of me the better to pick up my words of wisdom and impart them to the rest. It was rather a marvellous garden, I thought.

A writer of travelbooks in the 1920s and 1930s, JOHN GIBBONS started a journey in Barcelona which took him through Algarve and along the Portuguese coast north to Lisbon.

The Cathedral in Lagos

As far as I could see the principal business of everybody was to catch two small fish and then to sell them to somebody else. And as by that time everybody naturally had his or her own full complement, nobody particularly wanted them. Until in the end the original pair, a bit worse for wear with a day's chaffering and with being occasionally banged down on a dusty pavement, were dished up for my dinner. And I gave

Many fertile valleys can be found near Aljezur in the western foothills of the Serra de Monchique. The town holds an annual livestock market in early July. About three miles / five kilometres to the southwest is Praia da Arrifana, with the ruins of an ancient watch-tower. And to the northwest are the high sand-dunes of Praia de Clérigo.

Windmills, such as this thirteenth century example near Rogil with its conical walls and circular ground plan, are still a common sight in Algarve. Sometimes clay vessels are suspended from ends of the blades, omitting a whistling sound during rotation. When the sound stops, the owner knows that the wheel must be turned to face the wind.

the best part of them either to a beggar or a dog. I forget which, but both canines and humans come and beg impartially round the table in the eating-houses of that end of Portugal.

Then at the top of the cliff in Lagos you come to the ruins of an ancient Cathedral. It collapsed in some earthquake or other. But at the other end of the town there is another Cathedral, and quite near it stands a Church of Saint Anthony. When at last you find somebody to unlock the door and let you inside, the place is all gold. Or at least it looks like gold. And in the old days of the Royalty it was a very famous *Capella* indeed, and on Sundays and Great Days the military band from the garrison opposite would play there at High Mass. But now with the Republic of course all that is over, and as I say you've got to hunt up someone to unlock the door. But St. Anthony is still inside and a rather wonderful St. Anthony he is. Because before he went to Padua in Italy he was of course really a Portuguese and his countrymen were naturally proud of him. So a century or so after his death they made him an Honorary Captain-General in the Portuguese Army, and indeed it was rather wickedly said that some Bishop or other actually drew his pay for him. Then when a few hundred years later the Napoleonic Wars

came along, and we English were fighting in the Peninsula, the Portuguese as a sort of mutual bond of union suggested that we too might care to make the Saint an honorary officer in our Army as well. So that now the image of St. Anthony that you'll see in that *Capella* at Lagos is wearing a red sash over his monkly gown. And it is the sash of British Field-Officer rank of the early eighteen hundreds.

Also there was something else that I noticed in that gilded church. A monument to Senhor Hugo Beaty, Colonel of the Regiment Irlandez. As far as I could read the writing, it said that he was in life a Protestant but at the last became converted to the Catholic Church, Holy and Roman, so dying on the Second of December, 1789. And after that I motioned that I had seen all that I wanted and so left the cool darkness of that ancient and gorgeous Church for the dazzling blaze of the Square outside.

A tour in the early 1930s took JOHN GIBBONS from Barcelona to Lisbon, via Portugal's Algarve.

Prince Henry in Sagres

The old "Sacred Cape" of the Romans, then called Sagres, now the "Cape St. Vincent" of Nelson and

The lighthouse at the tip of Ponta da Piedade, a strip of land near Lagos with steep cliffs plunging into the sea. The building offers a superb view of the area's incomparable landscape of rocks and water.

modern maps, was [Prince Henry's] chosen home for the next forty years, though he seems to have passed a good deal of his time in his port of Lagos. …

The Sacred Cape, which he now colonised, was at any rate a good centre for his work of ocean voyaging. Here, with the Atlantic washing the land on three sides, he was well on the scene of action. There were buildings on Sagres headland as old as the eleventh century; Greek geography had made this the starting-point of its shorter and continental measurements for the length of the habitable world, and the Genoese, whose policy was to buy up points of vantage on every coast, were eager to plant a colony there, but Portugal was not ready to become like the Byzantine Empire, a depôt for Italian commerce, and Henry had his own reasons for securing a desolate promontory.

On this he now built himself a palace, a chapel, a study, an observatory – the earliest in Portugal – and a village for his helpers and attendants. "In his wish to gain a prosperous result for his efforts, the Prince devoted great industry and thought to the matter, and at great expense procured the aid of one Master Jacome from Majorca, a man skilled in the art of navigation and in the making of maps and instruments, and who was sent for, with certain of the Arab and Jewish mathematicians, to instruct the Portuguese in that science." So at least, says De Barros, the "Livy of Portugal." At Sagres was thus founded anew the systemic study of applied science in Christendom; it was better than the work of the old Greek "University" at Alexandria with which it has been compared, because it was essentially practical. From it "our sailors", says Pedro Nunes, "went out well taught and provided with instruments and rules which all mapmakers should know." We would gladly know more of Henry's scientific work; a good many legends have grown up about it, and even his foundation of the Chair of Mathematics in the University of Lisbon or Coimbra, our best evidence of the unrecorded work of his school, has been doubted by some modern critics, even by the national historian, Alexander Herculano. But to Prince Henry's study and science two great improvements on this side may be traced: first in the art of map-making, secondly in the building of caravels and ocean craft.

PRINCE HENRY THE NAVIGATOR (1394–1460) was the third son of King John I of Portugal and Philippa of Lancaster. According to some scholars, Henry's "navigational school" in Sagres never was established but is merely a tale. He did, however, promote the movement of explorers around the Atlantic.

The Sardine …

But abundance, riches, super-abundance is the sardine. It was inexhaustible, it was a solid mass, so much so that for whole nights in succession no one in Olhão was able to sleep. And it was said, today there was a great massacre of fish. Here there are two qualities; that of the south-east which comes in April and joins the shoals from the Morrocan coast; and the fish from the south-west, bigger, fatter, and less tasty, this without counting the sardine of passage which appears in January when it lays its eggs. "It's already getting lost" … say the fishermen, "The egg is biting it." It bites perhaps, perhaps the sardine scrapes its belly on the sand to make the skin finer, facilitating the delivery of the egg, because they arrive at this period at a depth of three fathoms. At Easter also it is certain. The sardine shoal goes swimming through this sea, and the boats and the young tunny, the men and the fish, rapacious, some at the tail, some at the head of that formidable silver cylinder, glut themselves night and day, fishing all the time, catching all the time, destroying all the time, without obliterating it.

The sardine comes shorewards every evening and retires in the morning. If there is a moon, it disappears. The boats sail with their lights dowsed in the heavy silence of these summer nights, in which the stars are reflected in the water like flashes of light and the wide milky-way lights up the sky and the sea at the same time with a vague whiteness. One or two wisps of vapour go by and sink. The master, Fadagulha, concentrated, waits … On board no one breathes, and it could be said that the other boats are also going on tip-toe. Silence and stars, more and more stars. And always this movement that I feel beneath my feet and this shoal that goes round me in concentric circles as the boat keeps changing position, under the sky that comes nearer and that I can feel heaving. The whole crew is alert, from the fishermen and the helmsmen to the stone-man and the master, who are the important persons on board. The master is not simply an observer, he is a magician. In order to cast the net, it is necessary to know not only where the fish are – and the master forecasts the shoal – but to calculate in advance the quality and quantity of the sardines that are going to be dragged in the cast, because it is not worth carrying out the manoeuvre for a small amount.

RAUL BRANDÃO (1867–1930) was one of the most original of Portuguese writers. His best writings reflect the people living either on the Atlantic coast or the coast of Algarve. Editor's Note: a stone-man was a fisherman who could avoid throwing the nets where the stones could cut or damage them.

… and the Tunny

The lad, after throwing a glance, half of shame, half of fear towards my group, began to strip off that quantity of rags in which the fishermen wrap themselves, even in summer, when they go to sea.

And he appeared exceptionally well-proportioned and strong, with a torso like a Greek breastplate, round in the chest and flat in the belly, with narrow hips, but with outstandingly muscular thighs. Except for his wrists, neck, and feet, all of which were sunburnt, he was as white as marble.

Standing up on the edge of the launch, raising his arms and putting his hands together, he swayed gently and then plunged into the water, diving down amongst the fish. But in a few seconds he emerged, almost at the opposite end of the boat, riding an enormous tunny, which, in order to rid itself of its strange burden, went twisting back into the water, jumping over the other fish that got in its way or diving suddenly to re-appear a few yards further off still with the Triton on its back, gripping a fin with his left hand, waving the other in the air and giving shouts of triumph. The lad was transfigured, he sparkled with daring and youth among the great salt waves of the reddish sea which was licking his body, and shone in the sun like living pink marble.

MANUEL TEIXEIRA GOMES (1860–1942) was one of the best writers about his home province, Algarve, along with Julio Dantas and the poet, João de Deus. Gomes served as Minister in London for some years.

The Countryside

More attractive than the towns is the Algarve countryside. The main road runs parallel to the sea between gardens, vineyards and orchards of orange, lemon, olive and fig. *O Algarve é pai do figo* runs an old adage, but if it is the father of the fig it is the child of the almond, and in early February, when the weather is generally pleasant, it is worth coming many miles to see the endless sea of tenuous blossom which stretches behind Faro and Tavira.

Some miles back from the coast run the smoke-blue mountains of Malhão and São Miguel, starred with white farmhouses, long, low buildings, each crowned with a tall decorative chimney of tile and plaster. All the pride and artistic taste of the peasants is put into these chimneys which, like slender white campaniles, lend every house the air of a chapel. In the plain there is often a miniature aqueduct, linking the water wheel with the house and with the garden where the young tomatoes are protected from the frost by aloe leaves bent double and spiked into the ground.

A typical inn in Albufeira. When the Portuguese get together, a shared meal is a must. Generally there are two warm meals each day, but the main evening meal, enjoyed with family or friends, takes precedence. In recent years, owing to the expanding tourist trade, the traditional cuisine has been expanded to include a number of foreign dishes.

Alte, a popular and picturesque mountain village lying east of Silves at the base of the Serra do Caldeirão.

Albufeira, the "Saint Tropez of Algarve", owes its nickname to many years as a favourite haunt of artists. The staggering number of bars and discotheques, catering to all tastes, bear witness to an impressive night-life.

There is no local costume, but the almond-eyed women, riding into town on mule-back, or filling their shapely water jars at the well, wear broad hats of heavy black felt over dark 'kerchiefs, a curiously becoming headgear. … As one follows the coast westwards past Lagos, a fresh, white little town, the soil grows more barren, and the landscape more arid. The distant *serras* fall away behind a foreground of low treeless hills. Soon, only the fig trees are left, and these bow ever lower before the strong winds from the west. …

At last, even the fig trees fail, and there is nothing but cistus scrub and stone. The contours flatten out, and the twin promontories of Sagres and St Vincent come into view, linked by a wide amphitheatre of vertical cliffs, stabbing the grey Atlantic. St Vincent, the extreme south-westerly corner of Europe, is marked only by a lighthouse. It is round the other headland that legend and tradition have gathered. In classical times Sagres was the Sacred Cape to which the gods came at night to rest from their journeyings. In Moorish times it was sanctified by a Christian church, and it was here that the relics of St Vincent came to shore guided and guarded by two holy crows.

RODNEY GALLOP is the author of several books on the folk culture of the Portuguese and Basques.

In the Sierra de Monchique

Towards the end of the day, with the work done and the sun dipping into the Western Atlantic, the old wind-mill above Alto is a good place to sit and contemplate the past and the future of human existence in this landscape. … Only a few years ago the miller used to sit here, waiting for the donkeys to haul grain up the mountain from Alto. Five hundred years earlier, the shepherd sat on the same spot, watching over his goats and sheep. Maybe a thousand years ago, a Moor sat here and looked across at his new fort.

… I was surrounded by Australian eucalyptus trees, imported into these mountains a mere twenty years ago. The miller was surrounded by sweet chestnuts, a few of which still remain – old, gnarled specimens with hollow trunks. The shepherd was undoubtedly surrounded by scrub, his goats and sheep having destroyed much of the vegetation on the mountain. And the Moor – what did he see? Probably an endless forest of cork oaks in all directions, with smaller scrub like the medronho trees nearer the dry tops of the mountains.

ROBIN JENKINS explored the soil of southern Portugal in a recent attempt at understanding the life-style of the people.

For centuries, Faro has been the seat of Algarve's Bishop. In front of the Cathedral is a statue to Francisco Gomes, the first Bishop of Faro. During a sixteenth century campaign, English troops made away with the Bishopric's Library, which formed the basis for Oxford's Bodleian Library.

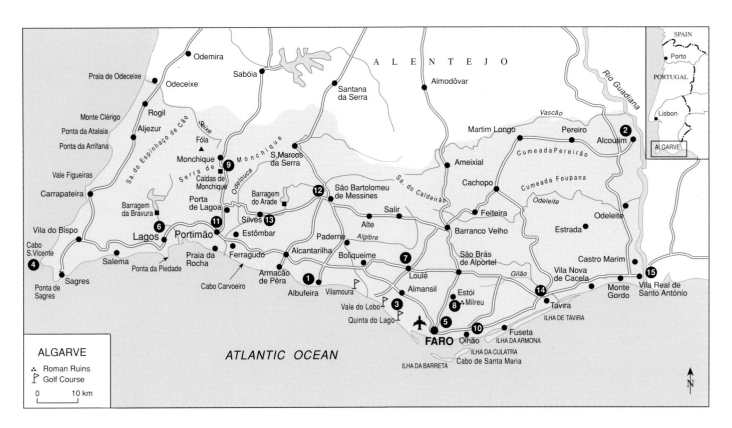

GENERAL INFORMATION

Algarve is the name given to the southern-most district of Portugal. For administrative purposes, the capital of the region is Faro. Algarve covers an area of 1,958 square miles / 5,072 square kilometres; it is bounded in the south and west by the Atlantic Ocean, in the east by the Guadiana River with separates it from Spain, and in the north by two mountain ranges, Serra de Monchique and Serra do Caldeirão. With mountain peaks rising between 1,800 and 2,700 feet / 600 and 900 metres, Algarve falls roughly into three geographic regions: the actual coastline (Beiramar) on which ninety percent of Algarvians live; a partly fertile and partly karstic area of hilly countryside (Barrocal); and the Serras, which are largely uninhabited. Confusion reigns as to whether the name should be given the definite article. In keeping with its Arabic root (*Al Gharb*, meaning "the west") and the Portuguese variant (*o Algarve*), the area should probably be called "the" Algarve. In English, however, it is referred to as Algarve.

INFORMATION

Região de Turismo do Algarve, Rua de Misericórdia 8 12, 8000 Faro. Tel.: (89) 21404-24067.

Practically every town in Algarve with tourist attractions has its own tourist office.

CLIMATE

Though Algarve lies at the same latitude as Sicily, it is governed by an Atlantic climate. This means that summer days are very hot (77° to 86° Fahrenheit / 25° to 30° Celsius) and the nights can become cool, particularly in the west. Temperatures are less extreme in the interior. The Barrocal region is very hot, while temperatures in the Serras become cooler with increasing altitude. Rainy days are rare and are usually only during the winter months and in the Serras. The water then flows to the coast, keeping the countryside green even during the hottest weather. Winters are comparatively mild, but sometimes stormy. One special event is the blossoming of the almond trees which occurs during January and February.

HOW TO GET THERE

There are many charter flights to Faro, especially during the summer. Regularly scheduled flights are offered by Lufthansa and the Portuguese airlines TAP. Most rail connections pass either through Paris or Lisbon. An inexpensive but exhausting

bus trip from Cologne to Lisbon (44 hours long!) is offered by Deutsche Touring. During the summer months, three to four days should be added to the time of the journey. The shortest routes from the north are via Paris and Madrid, from the south through Barcelona.

TRANSPORT

The most common means of local transportation in Portugal are the buses of "Rodoviária Nacional" which travel even to small and remote localities. The relatively long journeys are made bearable by bus as opposed to the antiquated railway, "Comboio", which departs from a suburban station on the other side of the Tejo River in Lisbon. The most comfortable means of travel is still motorcar, though the traffic jams on the coastal highway can be frustrating. Traffic regulations are the same as elsewhere in Europe. The maximum speed limits are 200 miles / 120 kilometres per hour on motorways, 150 miles / 90 kilometres per hour on country roads, and 36 miles / 60 kilometres per hour within town limits.

CURRENCY

The national currency of Portugal is the escudo; coins of smaller denominations (centavos) are seldom used. As well, coins of 2½ and 25 escudos exist, but are unusual. Banknotes are available from 50 to 5,000 escudos, the latter often being difficult to break. Theoretically the escudo is freely convertible within the Common Market; it is however, difficult to re-exchange even within Portugal.

Credit cards are widely accepted in tourist regions and larger shops. However, you should not rely on them when travelling in the interior of Algarve.

The Fish Market in Monchique.

FOOD AND DRINK

An international fare has taken hold in Algarve's holiday areas. Nonetheless, there is still ample opportunity to sample the distinctive and tasty Portuguese cuisine, particular in the region's interior. Typical of Algarve, and well-known abroad, is *cataplana*, pork which has been roasted with mussels in a closed metal pot; the dish is also known as *carne alentejana*. Other specialities include several stews: a rich fish chowder called *caldeirada*, a mixture of beans (*favas*) and countless dishes prepared with cod (*bacalhau*). Another typical fare comes from the north: *caldo verde*, a soup made of potatoes and cabbage.

Fish, of course, are a staple, especially the *sardinha*. Sardines are particularly tasty when rubbed with sea salt, roasted over a charcoal grill and served with local red wine and coarse bread; they are often cooked in this manner at open-air restaurants and during village festivals. Other

popular seafoods are swordfish (*espada*) and squid (*lulas*). The less common species especially shellfish, are more expensive.

The Portuguese are rather unaccustomed to meat dishes, which may explain the sometimes arbitrary choices. In general, one is on safe ground with the thinly sliced, pan-fried cuts known as *febras*.

There is no shortage of desserts on offer in Portugal. If you want to avoid *flan*, the standard caramel pudding, there are many types of *bolos* (cakes) and occasionally *doces* (sweets) to be had. The latter are often made from local crops including figs and almonds and sold by street vendors. The most important beverage, of course, is wine. Many restaurateurs have their own special brand which is poured directly into the carafe from large wicker-covered bottles, though the latter, unfortunately, are increasingly yielding to plastic. According to popular opinion, the best wine is *Dão*, but less well-known southern brands should also be sampled. One specialty of the region is *vinho verde* which is the product of young grapes growning at high altitudes. It is very light, tart, and slightly effervescent. Although native to northern Portugal, the wine is perfect for a hot day in Algarve. No full meal is complete without a demitasse of strong mocca (*bica*) and a glass of brandy, either *bagaceira* (a wine liqueur often added directly to the coffee!) or *medronho* (see page 36). And this is followed by a well-earned siesta.

SOUVENIRS

Keepsakes for family and friends are found to abundance and at good prices. One popular souvenir is the glazed dishware of red clay offered in large quantities at every market. It is more solid than it looks, and can generally be put through the dishwasher. There are also other types of ceramics available including glazed tiles. Figurines often take the form of the rooster, the national symbol of Portugal. One should also forget the large vases and chimneys (see page 20) which can be bought at roadside stands but which can quickly exceed luggage limits.

Being a peasant nation rich in traditions, handicrafts of all sorts continue to flourish in present-day Portugal. Despite Common Market regulations, hand-made goods are relatively inexpensive, provided the

requisite materials are locally available. Baskets, hats and dolls are woven from straw, raffia and reeds. The coarse Algarvian wool is used to knit pullovers, jackets and caps; clothing and linen are often

A market-day conversation in Monchique.

colourfully embroidered. More expensive gifts include items of brass or copper, specialities from the town of Loulé. All of these can also be found at the airport in Faro and the souvenir shops of tourist hotels. But it is more entertaining, and less expensive, to buy them at local markets (*mercados*), where bargaining is still allowed.

A SHORT GLOSSARY

AZULEJOS. The connoisseur's term for the decorative glazed tiles adorning many churches and other buildings. Interesting azulejo designs often surround the public fountains found in most Algarvian towns (see page 20).

BARROCAL. The hilly countryside located between the seacoast and the Serra Mountains.

CORK. Though the majority of Portugal's cork comes from Alentejo, Algarve also has noteworthy stands of cork trees as far south as the Barrocal. The trees are easily recognized by their trunks: the bark will have been peeled off as high as the first branch, exposing the reddish brown wood. The process does little damage to the tree, however, for the bark will grow back within five to ten years, after which it will be peeled off again. The bark is processed in small factories, producing not only corks but also souvenirs of all sorts, from place-mats to ties and postcards.

MEDRONHO. A popular liqueur distilled from the fruit of the "strawberry tree", which is found growing naturally in Algarve's mountainous regions.

MISERICÓRDIA is the name (meaning compassion) given to those churches which, in medieval times, were attached to the state-supported hospitals and clinics.
In the building interiors, it is possible to find pictures of the fourteen principal acts of compassion. One such church is located in Tavira.

POUSADA. The Portuguese name for those state-run hotels which, like the *paradores* in Spain, are situated in scenically or architecturally remarkable locations. In many examples, historic building are used, and thus preserved. Most have a venerable elegance. As they are also relatively inexpensive (but not necessarily cheap!), it is not easy to secure accommodation without an advance reservation. However, you can simply stop by to enjoy a tasty meal or to drink a cup of coffee. To be recommended are the *São Brás* in São Brás de Alportel, the *Pousada do Infante* in Sagres, and the *Pousada de Santa Clara* positioned, in Santa Clara-a-Velha on the banks of a reservoir in the Monchique mountains.

ROSSIO. In practically all Portuguese towns, this is the popular name given to the town square, no matter what its official name, which is usually unfamiliar to the locals, may be.

TALHA DOURADA is the Portuguese term for woodcarvings found on church altars and interiors, usually covered with gold. They are a reminder of the extravagant eighteenth century and its wealth of precious metals from Brazil.

TOURADA. In this, the Portuguese version of bullfighting, no blood is shed. In keeping with the Portuguese character, the object of the sport is to face the bull unarmed. Seven men advance toward the animal while an eighth tries to grasp on to the tail.

POINTS OF INTEREST

The circled numbers refer to the map on page 48; those in italics refer to the colour photographs.

ALBUFEIRA ①. This town with a population of 10,000 is the centre of Algarve's tourist industry. Albufeira has also attracted much attention through its trade and commerce. As its main streets are often congested by traffic, it is better to walk though the smaller side streets which have preserved the small-town character of earlier times. Albufeira's history dates back to the Romans and Moors (its name comes from *al-buaira*, the Arabic word for lagoon); the town continued to be of some significance during Portugal's early days. Little remains of this history, however, as most of Albufeira's structures were destroyed either during the earthquake of 1755 or the civil wars. The most important remaining monument is the sixteenth century *Capela da Misericórdia*. The *Church of St Sebastian*, somewhat to the west, is also of interest: one portal is in the Renaissance style while another follows the Manueline trend.
As it is enclosed by rocky cliffs, the beautiful beach near Albufeira can be accessed by a tunnel some 150 feet / 50 metres long. Fishermen still dock here in the evenings and offer their wares for sale at the fish market to the east. *7, 43, 46*
The town environs, especially the beaches further to the east (*Vilamoura, Quarteira* and *Vale do Lobo*), are among the most heavily developed tourist areas in the country. Here there are rows of large hotels and holiday resorts, interspersed by small inns, golf courses and an enormous yacht harbour near Quarteira.

ALCOUTIM ②. This is the only town to be situated on the north bank of the Guadiana River. Alcoutim is, therefore, located in one of the most remote corners of the province. At one time, the settlement was strategically important in Portugal's conflict with Spain: it had an impressive harbour in which goods for the entire hinterland arrived from across the river. Today, with 5,000 residents, Alcoutim exists on the basis of the agricultural yields of the surrounding countryside and the fishing of the Guadiana where eels, especially, are harvested. Alcoutim has virtually no contact with the Spanish town of

Sanlúcar on the opposite bank of the river. The town has largely been overlooked by tourists and is recommended to all who favour unspoiled solitude. *15*

ALMANSIL ③. It is worth visiting this tiny spot between Albufeira and Faro to see *São Lourenço de Matos*, a church whose interior is almost entirely covered with azulejo murals. A lovely altar of talha dourada (gilt

São Lourenço de Matos in Almansil.

woodcarvings) dominates the splendid blue and white tiles which extend to the cupola. Opposite the church is a privately run cultural centre, perhaps the most important of its kind in Algarve. *21*

CABO SÃO VINCENTE and **SAGRES** ④. Located at the southernmost tip of Portugal, Cabo São Vincente and the neighbouring town of Sagres are set in a forbidding landscape. This high plateau has an impressive beauty: its steep cliff faces plunge breathtakingly into the sea. A beautiful view can be had from the lighthouse at the tip of the cape; though a minimal entrance fee is charged, the technology of this 144 year-old structure, the most powerful lighthouse in Europe, is rather impressive. On *Ponta de Sagres*, the rocky plateau towering over the sea near Sagres, Henry the Navigator is said to have founded his legendary "maritime school" during the fifteenth century. Today the fortified walls (renovated in the seventeenth century) enclose a few buildings which have been heavily restored. They are frequently used to house exhibits on the Age of Discoveries; there is also a daily screening of a somewhat overly dramatized film on Portugal's expeditions.

Sagres itself is a modest town offering few diversions except for the many restaurants and cafés which are located beside the harbour as well as a new hotel, the Pousada

A view of the Old Town in Albufeira.

do Infante. *Raposeira*, (meaning foxhole), the residence of Prince Henry, is located six miles / ten kilometres to the north near Vila do Bispo. Just over one mile / two kilometres to the east of the home is a small pathway leading to one of the earliest sacred buildings in the region, the chapel *Nossa Senhora da Guadeloupe*, where Henry is said to have prayed. To see the interior, ask the sacristan for the key.

CASTRO MARIM. See under Vila Real de Santo António.

ESTÓI. See under Milreu.

FARO ⑤**.** The largest city (pop. 30,000) and administrative capital of the Algarve district was known in ancient times as Ossonoba. As Faro's harbour is protected at sea by sandbars, it can be accessed only via a lagoon. A walk through the busy town centre is best begun at this small, picturesque *harbour*. Faro also fell victim to the 1755 earthquake and few historical buildings survived. Still, the *pedestrian mall*, with its geometric cobblestone pat-

terns, is ideally suited for passing the time of day. The most impressive structure is *Sé Cathedral*, located on Largo da Sé, a broad and peaceful plaza. Like most Gothic cathedrals in Portugal, it was originally built to look like a fortress. Only the tower has survived from the original structure; the other parts of the building were added later in a variety of styles, including the late Baroque which is otherwise rare in

Along the fortified walls of the Nossa Senhora da Graça Chapel in Ponta de Sagres.

Algarve. Another building to have survived the earthquake is the *Clarissine Convent* (completed in 1543) with its two storeyed cloister. Today it contains an archeological museum named after Prince Henry (open Tuesday to Sunday, 10:00 am to noon, and 2:00 to 5:00 pm). Those

interested in Portugal's overseas discoveries should also visit the *Museu Marítimo Ramalho Ortigão* at the Port Authority (Capitania do Porto): here there are models of all the country's famous exploratory vessels in addition to an exhibition on Algarve's fishing industry (open Monday to Friday, 9:00 am to 12:30 pm and 2:00 to 5:30 pm, and half days on Saturday). If you have some time to spare, you might consider visiting the Baroque *Carmelite Church* in the northern part of town, the nearby sixteenth century Church of *São Pedro* with its azulejo murals, or, east of the cathedral, the *Franciscan Church*, which also has decorative tiles. *47*

Lagos' monument to Henry the Navigator.

LAGOS ⑥**.** This town of 7,000 residents has been surrounded by a wall since Roman times when it was called Lacobriga. Lagos's importance peaked during the fifteenth century, when Henry the Navigator based his shipyards here and also hired sailors for his expeditions from the town (see page 19). Lagos' points of interest, all located on the harbour, date from this period: the *fortress*, the *slave market*

As visitors soon notice, there is something "English" about Algarve, and for that matter, with the whole of Portugal. This is not coincidental: as countries with historically widespread mercantile empires, England and Portugal became natural allies of a sort. In 1703, this bond was recognized in the Methuen Treaty, a document regulating trade relations and the exchange of port wine and English woolens. The fiery southern temperament has been diluted with English discipline, causing the Portuguese to queue patiently at bus stops, among other things. The English influence can also be seen in the telephone booths and mail boxes, the so-called "pillar boxes".

But nature also has contributed to the Englishness of the region. Owing to the Atlantic climate, the countryside is green throughout the year and it is not difficult to maintain a lawn area. Algarve, then, is ideal for sports such as horseback riding, cricket, and most especially, golf. Between Quarteira, Vilamoura and Albufeira, there are still spots where the pine forests and grass extend to the steep cliffs of the coast. Pedestrians and equestrians have these areas largely to themselves, and at most are likely to meet a solitary golfer at the edge of a green.

Algarve hosts many sports-oriented vacations. The higher quality and more established hotels, such as Alpha Mar in Vale do Lobo, offer all manner of services, not only on the hotel grounds but, thanks to special arrangements, in local facilities as well. And this has not only attracked the English, for whom a season in Algarve, at a time when the rest of the region was an

HORSEBACK RIDING AND GOLF AMONG GREEN CLIFFS

Tourist offices and hotels can provide ready information on sporting holidays, particularly involving the Algarve's special pride, its golf courses. In total there are six: Quinta do Lago near Faro, Penina near Portimão, Palmares near Lagos, and,

The golf course in Vale do Lobo. The seventh green is played along the rocky coastline.

uncharted enigma, had a touch of snob appeal. The trend toward active holidays has reinforced the natural offerings of Algarve's landscape and temperate climate, allowing hotel owners to lengthen the tourist season.

in close proximity to each other, Vilamoura, Dom Pedro and Vale do Lobo in the tourist centres east of Albufeira. And as visitors automatically excel to the ranks of Algarvian nobility, few conditions need to be met to gain access to the greens.

and the *Governor's Palace* with the window of King Sebastian (see page 28) who briefly made Lagos the capital of Algarve. Most likely because it bore the same name as the king, the *Chapel of St Sebastian* was expanded over the course of the sixteenth century to become a church; the structure was restored after the 1755 earthquake. The narrow streets leading to the church are also worth exploring. Visitors should also see *Santo António*, a church which appears modest from the outside but whose interior is heavily decorated with the gold imported to Portugal during the eighteenth century from Brazil. Lagos has a small *Regional Museum* (open Tuesday

to Sunday, 9:30 am to 12:30 pm and 2:00 to 5:00 pm) containing Roman artefacts as well as implements and handicrafts from the vicinity. *23*

All visitors to Lagos should make an excursion to *Ponta da Piedade*, a rocky beach that the insurgent sea has turned into bizarre reddish-yellow shapes, including a rock bridge. Ponta da Piedade can be reached either by boat or swimming. Nothing surpasses the view obtained from the scenic lookout known as Dona Ana. *22, 24, 25, 27, 49*

LOULÉ ⑦. Inland from Faro is the small town of Loulé (pop. 16,000), the centre of

a busy agricultural region in the Barrocal. Though often overlooked, Loulé has one of the earliest *parish churches* (matriz) in Algarve, dating from the eighth century. The majestic simplicity of the exterior, however, stands in sharp contrast to the stylistic eclecticism of the interior. The side chapels on the left, São Brás and Das Almas, merit a closer look due to their decorative tiles. Equally worth visiting is the *Misericórdia Church* which has a Manueline portal that has been extended with Renaissance elements. *10*

Loulé is also an important pilgrimage site: the simple chapel *Nossa Senhora da Piedade*, known locally as *Mãe Soberana*,

A landscape on the way to the Serra do Caldeirão, north from Faro near Loulé.

On the outskirts of the nearby town of *Estói*, with its pretty church, is a small palace dating from the end of the thirteenth century; the grounds boast a romantically overgrown pleasure garden. The charm of the ensemble lies in its three-tiered layout: the avenue (its regular design is still detectable), the ascending rotunda with a moss-covered fountain and busts, and finally the palace itself, which is closed to visitors. In both Milreu and Estói unofficial tour guides, usually a gardener or watchman, are easily found. Their explanations are peppered with anecdotes ranging from amusing to hair-raising. *33*

has been given a modern domed annex which is still awaiting completion. The site offers a lovely view of the town, which is attractive not so much for its churches as for its handicrafts and cottage artisans. Here you can still admire traditional hand-made folk art (including reddish-brown earthen ware) sold in small shops or at the artist's home, but especially at the rural market on weekends. Loulé is also renown for its fine examples of decorative chimneys.

carob trees vie with fields and hedges. In the town itself, you should climb to the like-named pousada and enjoy the view of the town and countryside. Nearby are two remarkable points of interest.

Though somewhat neglected, *Milreu*, the largest roman remains in Algarve, is interesting for the thermal baths in the ground-level excavations. Beside it, and difficult to overlook, are the ruins of a Romanesque basilica; little is known of the church's history, though local tour guides offer

Statues in the palace gardens in Estói.

A garden staircase at the palace in Estói decorated with azulejos.

MILREU, ESTÓI and **SÃO BRÁS DE ALPORTEL** ⑧. The rural town of *São Brás* is especially attractive for its surrounding landscape, where stands of almond, cork and

their own explanation. The sweltering excavation site has a charm all its own. Milreu can only be reached comfortably by motorcar.

MONCHIQUE ⑨. The little spa *Caldas de Monchique*, lying amidst the highest mountains in Algarve, is worth visiting not only for the bygone grandeur of its Belle Epoque architecture but also for its luxuriant natural setting and the scenic views from the peaks and plateaus. On the same road leading to the Monchique, you pass through the *Barranco* (Canyon) *dos Pisões*, one of the loneliest and wildest landscapes in Portugal, to arrive at *Odeceixe*, a little fishing village near the Algarve border, whose buildings convey the impression of an Alentejo town. A more hospitable road can carry you back from Odeceixe to Lagos or even to Cabo

São Vincente. This unusual but rewarding round-trip presents a side of Algarve off the beaten tourist path; two or three days should be set aside for it. *36*

OLHÃO ⑩. The crowded centre of this town now is often cited as a prime example of the ground plan and architectural style of the Muslim *medina* (old town) to have survived in southern Portugal. For confirmation of this, one need only wander through its tortuous alleyways, absorbing the atmosphere of the massive white buildings with their tiny windows, colourful courtyards and rooftop gardens. Surprisingly, Olhão did not come into existence until 1698, the year the parish church was completed, and thus, gives striking proof of the continued existence of Muslim traditions in Christian Algarve centuries after the Reconquista.

The recent confusion of architectural additions surrounding the old town has helped Olhão to shed its role as a typical Algarvean town. It now has a population of 20,000. Visitors in search of a more authentic atmosphere often prefer *Fuseta*, a quieter but similarly laid out town a few kilometres to the east.

PORTIMÃO ⑪. The Phoenicians and Carthaginians were among the first to make use

At the Praia da Rocha, near Portimão.

of this safe harbour at the mouth of the Arade River. Yet little if anything has survived of Portimão's ancient history: the earthquake of 1755 reduced also this town to rubble. As with Vila Real, Portimão's importance for western Algarve revolves around its turn of the century sardine canning industry and the tourist trade on the surrounding beaches.

Today, apart from the lovely portal of its parish church, Portimão offers little more than a simple shopping town of 28,000

In the harbour city of Portimão.

The twelfth-century Cathedral in Silves.

In Olhão, east of Faro. The eighteenth-century Old Town is particularly interesting.

residents. There is an appealing cobble-stone pedestrian mall and with it, daunting traffic congestion.

Its beach, however, the *Praia da Rocha*, has been the cradle of Algarve's tourist trade from a days when the region was visited only by affluent English travellers. The beach extends for several kilometres, offering a succession of hotels and private residences along the sand and rocks of the coastline. Some of the rock formations are famous, including the "three brothers" which rises up from the sea as well as several caves which can be investigated at low tide.

SAGRES. See under Cabo São Vincente.

SÃO BARTOLOMEU DE MESSINES ⑫. Most travellers arriving from Lisbon consider São Bartolomeu, a town of 10,000 set in the foothills of the Serra do Caldeirão, to be little more than the entryway to Algarve. This does it an injustice: visitors should note the pretty fifteenth century *Manueline Church* located on a hilltop in the town's centre.

São Bartolomeu is a typical Algarvean town. Though it has suffered somewhat from its location at a major highway intersection, the town is surrounded by well tended farmland which offers complete solitude, as on, for example, the shores of *Arade Reservoir.*

In Tavira. Above: Elaborate homes in the former capital. Below: A Moorish-style home.

SÃO BRÁS DE ALPORTEL. See under Milreu.

SILVES ⑬. Formerly the capital of Muslim Algarve, Silves is now a country town of 10,000 residents situated in the Barrocal. Its mighty *double walls*, topped by a footpath, recall a glorious past. Another wall, which once protected the lower town and was joined to a system of aqueducts, has been razed to the ground. Excavations beneath the Moorish castle have unearthed ancient cisterns and traces of other buildings dating as far back as Roman times. The twelfth century *Romanesque-Gothic Cathedral* is the oldest in Algarve.

Built on the site of a mosque, it has survived in its original form, apart from some minor earthquake damage. Just outside the town to the north is a fifteenth century roadside cross of carved limestone, set at an intersection. This is the *Cruz de Portugal*, so-called because of its function as a signpost for travellers to Portugal, which was already a separate political entity at the time of its construction. *16, 30, 31*

TAVIRA ⑭. Even under the Moors, Tavira was an important town as can be seen from the ruins of its town wall and the Church of Santa Maria, erected on the foundations of an ancient mosque. Tavira was conquered by the Knights of St James in 1242. History relates that the Moors broke a temporary truce by ambushing a hunting party of Christians (the seven victims are buried in the cathedral). This event served as a pretext for the *fúria cristiana*, the wrath of the crusaders during and after the siege. Tavira, too, was damaged heavily by the earthquake of 1755. Like Vila Real, though less systematically, it was rebuilt by the Marquês de Pombal to become an important fishing harbour. Most of its old buildings date from the reconstruction, as do the picturesque alleyways between the Praça da República and the Muslim ruins which give Tavira its nostalgic charm. *45*

In front of the church in Castro Marim. The fourteenth century fortress is also worth visiting.

Tavira has many churches. One of the most striking has already been mentioned: the hilltop church of *Santa María do Castelo*. Like many other Portuguese churches, it was also meant to be a place of defense and refuge, which accounts for its massive and imposing Gothic design. The Manueline additions date from a later period. Tavira also has a Misericórdia church (built in 1541), the most beautiful of its kind in Algarve; it has a remarkable two-colour Renaissance portal, gilt wood-carvings and tile murals in the interior.

The main square of this town of 13,000 residents is the Praça da República. From here, a *Roman bridge* leads over the Gilão River, which winds through the canals and lagoons of the outlying estuary to reach the open sea. Especially during the nineteenth century, Tavira was the focal point of the annual tuna harvest as well as the Tuna Exchange where the catch was auctioned. Due to its difficult access, especially for deep keeled ships, the harbour in Tavira eventually gave way in importance to others, above all that in Olhão.

VILA REAL DE SANTO ANTÓNIO and CASTRO MARIM ⑮.

Vila Real, a town of 11,000 residents on the border with Spain, has a town plan of un-Portuguese regularity (see page 31). The town is quickly and easily explored, after which visitors will most likely direct their attention to the surrounding area. There are long sandy beaches, hotels and campsites around the torrid *Monte Gordo*, which unlike the sheltered beaches to the west, lies on the open sea. But the region also involves the quiet flow of the Guadiana, a navigable river which can be explored by boat. The river initially flows through flat marshy land, a haven for many species of water fowl. Tributaries and canals lead to smaller villages such as *Odeleite* in the north.

The most important town along the Guadiana is *Castro Marim* (pop. 6,000), an elevation in the swampland whose stra-

A blooming fig cactus near Castro Marim.

tegic advantages were appreciated by the Phoenicians. This town used to lie on the border between Christian and Muslim territory, hence its mighty *fortress* built in the fourteenth century, the first seat of the Knights of Christ. In the wetlands between the town and railway line, there is a nature reserve called *Sapal*; it offers refuge to water animals of all sorts, including birds such as storks which find an ample supply of food here. Eastern Algarve thus ends in an area linked ecologically with the broad swamplands of southern Spain.

LIST OF SOURCES

C. Raymond Beazley, *Prince Henry the Navigator. The Hero of Portugal and of Modern Discovery, 1394–1460 A. D.* London: G. P. Putnam's Sons, 1931.

Raul Brandão, "The Sardine", in *Portugal Through Her Literature. An Anthology of Prose and Verse.* Edited by A. R. Barter. Translation of the excerpt "A Sardinha", from *Os Pescadores,* by A. R. Barter. Glastonbury: Walton Press, n. d.

Rodney Gallop, *Portugal: A Book of Folk-Ways.* Cambridge: Cambridge University Press, 1961.

John Gibbons, *Afoot in Portugal.* London: Georges Newnes, Limited, 1933.

Manuel Teixeira Gomes, "The Tunny Fishers", in *Portugal Through Her Literature. An Anthology of Prose and Verse.* Edited by A. R. Barter. Translation of the excerpt "Os pescadores de atum", from *Uma Copejada de Atum,* by A. R. Barter. Glastonbury: Walton Press, n. d.

Robin Jenkins, *The Road to Alto. An Account of Peasants, Capitalists and the Soil in the Mountains of Southern Portugal.* London: Pluto Press, 1979.

Dan Stanislawski, *Portugal's Other Kingdom. The Algarve.* Houston: University of Texas Press, 1963. Copyright © 1963, by permission of the University of Texas Press.

We would like to thank all copyright holders for their kind permission to reprint. Those we were not able to reach are asked to contact us.

LIST OF ILLUSTRATIONS

Bavaria Bildagentur, Gauting: page 52.

Jan Bode: pages 2, 4/5, 10, 14/15, 20 upper, 29, 41, 43, 44/45, 47, 49, 51 upper, 53 left, 54 middle, 56 lower.

Ruth Engels: back cover, pages 6/7, 9, 11, 36, 37, 40, 50, 53 upper and lower left, 54 upper, 56 upper.

Ministerio da Cultura e Coordenção Cintifica, Lisbon: page 12.

Cornelius Weber: front cover, pages 13, 16–19, 20 left and lower, 21–26/27, 30–34/35, 39, 46, 51 upper, 53 right, 54 lower, 55.

The map on page 48 was drawn by Astrid Fischer, Munich.

DESTINATION ALGARVE
WINDSOR BOOKS INTERNATIONAL, 1992

© 1992 by Verlag C. J. Bucher GmbH, Munich and Berlin
Translation: Bradford Robinson
Editor: Karen Lemiski
Anthology: David Lemiski

All rights reserved
Printed and bound in Germany
ISBN 1 874111 09 X